Leckie
the education publisher
for Scotland

Primary Maths
for Scotland

1st Level Maths

1A

Practice Workbook 2

Author: Kirsten MacKay
Series Consultant: Carol Lyon
Series Editor: Craig Lowther

001/10102024

10 9 8 7 6 5 4 3 2 1

ISBN 9780008680282

Published by
Leckie
An imprint of HarperCollins Publishers
Westerhill Road, Bishopbriggs, Glasgow, G64 2QT

T: 0844 576 8126 F: 0844 576 8131
leckiescotland@harpercollins.co.uk www.leckiescotland.co.uk

HarperCollins Publishers
Macken House, 39/40 Mayor Street Upper, Dublin 1, D01 C9W8, Ireland

Publisher: Fiona McGlade

Special thanks
Project editor: Peter Dennis
Layout: Siliconchips
Proofreader: Julianna Dunn

A CIP Catalogue record for this book is available from the British Library.

Acknowledgements
Images © Shutterstock.com

Printed in the UK by Martins the Printers

This book contains FSC™ certified paper and other controlled sources to ensure responsible forest management.

For more information visit: www.harpercollins.co.uk/green

Contents

Answers
Check your answers to this workbook online: https://collins.co.uk/pages/scottish-primary-maths

5.1 Make and identify halves

1 Tick the shapes that have been cut in half.

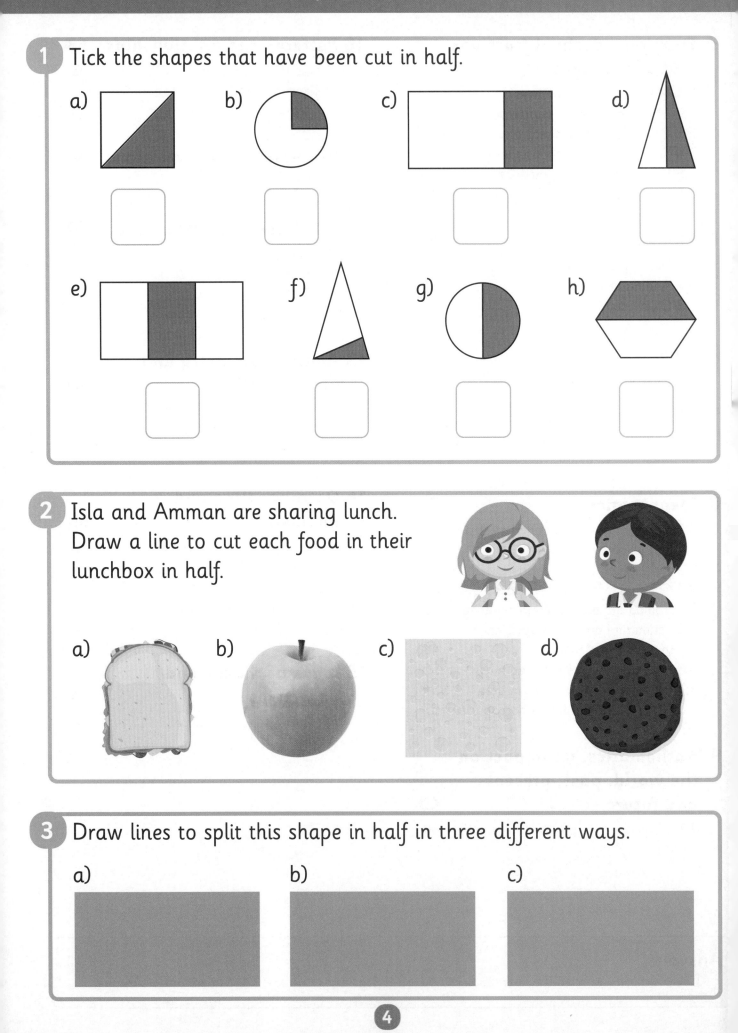

a)

b)

c)

d)

e)

f)

g)

h)

2 Isla and Amman are sharing lunch. Draw a line to cut each food in their lunchbox in half.

a)

b)

c)

d)

3 Draw lines to split this shape in half in three different ways.

a)

b)

c)

4 Nuria made playdough shapes. She cut each one in half to share with Finlay. Finlay doesn't think Nuria's halves are fair. Tick the shapes that have been cut in half. Write a cross if you think they are not halves.

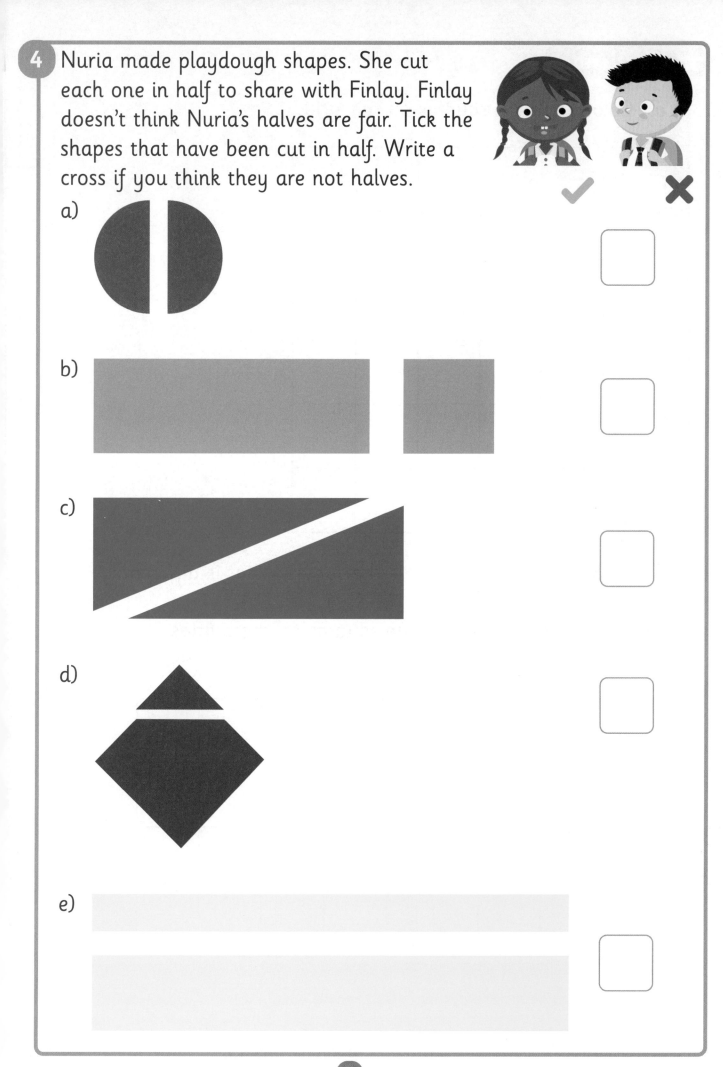

a)

b)

c)

d)

e)

a) Colour half the squares on this grid.

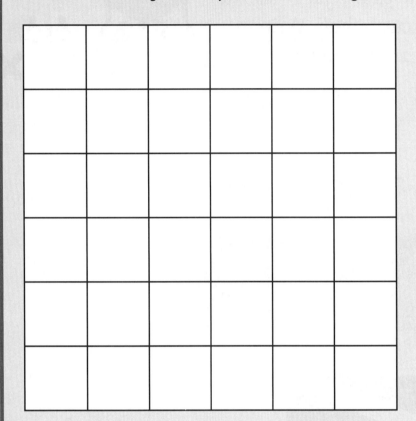

Share with a partner. What is the same? What is different?

b) Now try colouring half the squares on these grids in different ways.

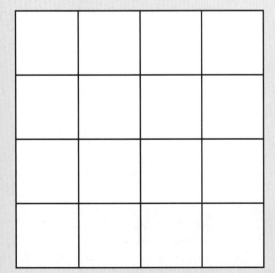
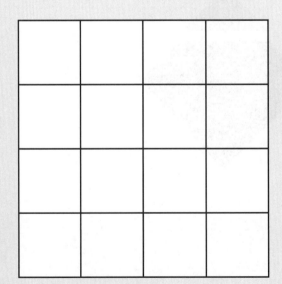

5.2 Make and identify quarters

1 Tick the shapes that have been cut into quarters.

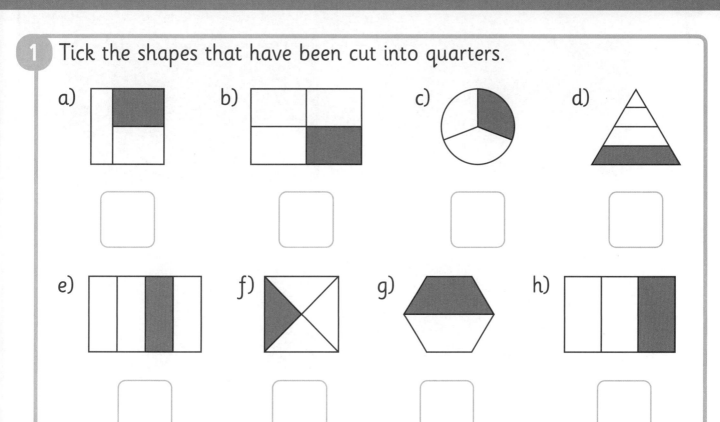

a)   b)   c)   d)

e)   f)   g)   h)

2 Draw lines on each food to cut it into quarters.

a)

b)

c)

d)
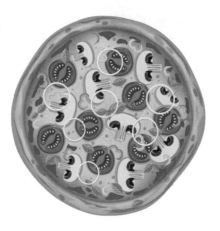

3 Draw lines to split this shape into quarters in four different ways.

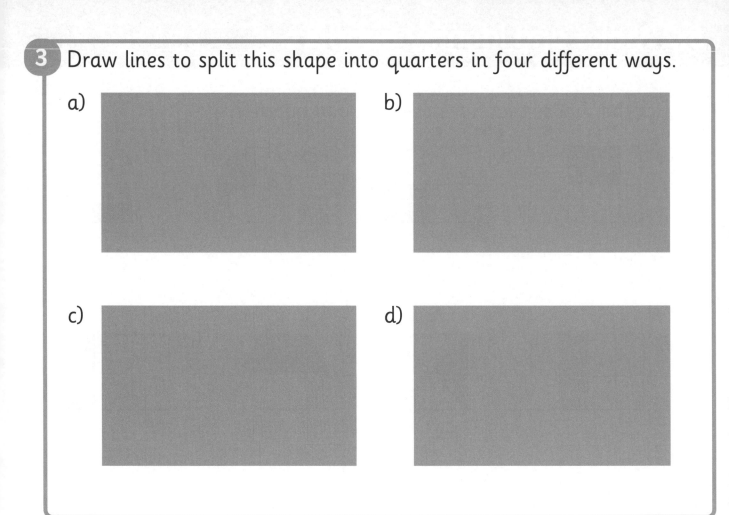

a)

b)

c)

d)

★ **Challenge**

a) Isla says she has cut this shape into quarters and coloured one quarter.

Finlay thinks Isla is wrong. He cut the shape into quarters and coloured one quarter like this.

Who is correct?

b) Is there another way you could cut this shape into quarters? Draw lines to split it into quarters and colour one quarter.

1 Nuria cuts whole apples in half.
How many halves does Nuria have?

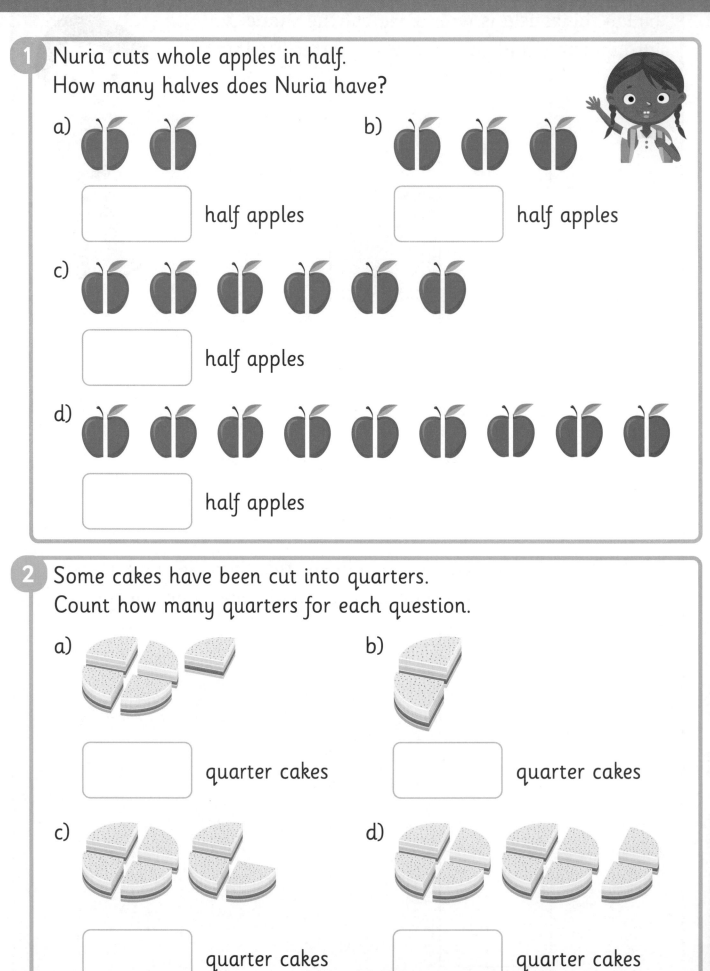

a)

[ ] half apples

b)

[ ] half apples

c)

[ ] half apples

d)

[ ] half apples

2 Some cakes have been cut into quarters.
Count how many quarters for each question.

a)

[ ] quarter cakes

b)

[ ] quarter cakes

c)

[ ] quarter cakes

d)

[ ] quarter cakes

3 Count in halves or quarters and write how many altogether.

a)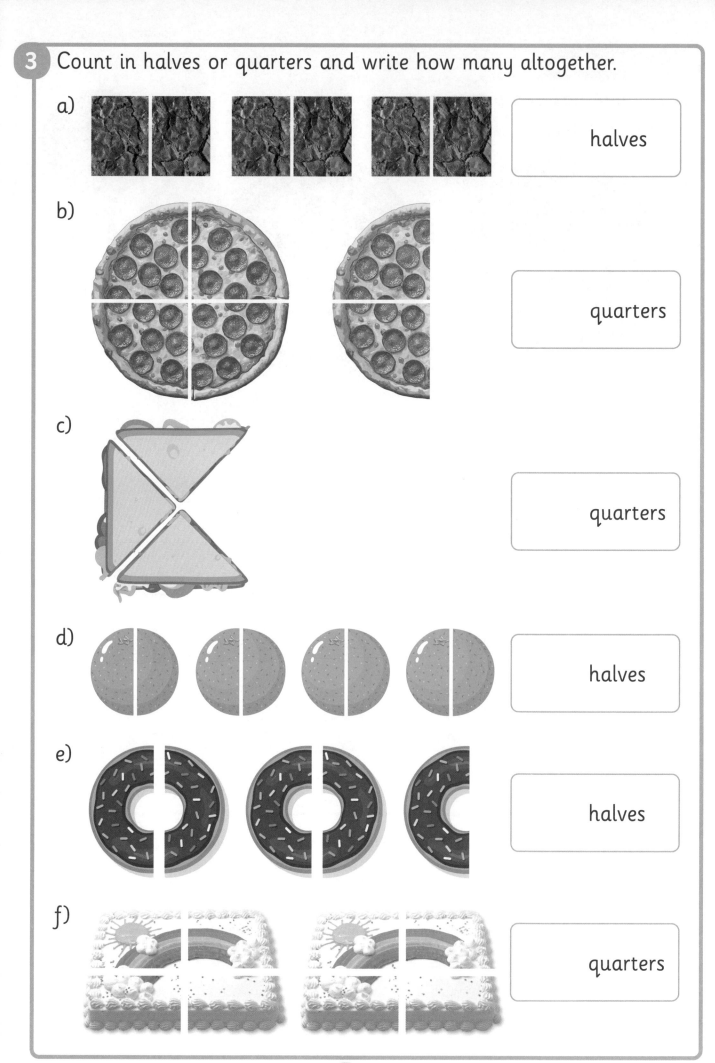

halves

b)

quarters

c)

quarters

d)

halves

e)

halves

f)

quarters

11

Amman has two pizzas and cuts each one into quarters.

 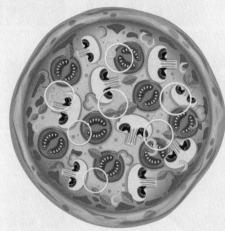 

a) How many quarters will there be altogether? Draw lines on each pizza to help you work it out.

b) Amman's family eat five quarters. How much will be left?

1 Isla and Amman have shared some fruit between them.
Have they shared the fruit fairly?
Tick **yes** or **no**.

a)

yes	no
☐	☐

b)

yes	no
☐	☐

c)

yes	no
☐	☐

d)

yes	no
☐	☐

2

a) 6 pencils shared equally between 3 pots gives?

☐ ☐ ☐

b) 8 pencils shared equally between 2 pots gives?

☐ ☐

c) 10 pencils shared equally between 5 pots gives?

d) 12 pencils shared equally between 4 pots gives?

---

3 a) Share 6 marbles equally between 3 children.

How many marbles will each child get?

b) Share 12 pencils equally between 2 pots.

How many pencils in each pot?

c) Share 20 cars equally between 5 garages.

How many cars in each garage?

d) Share 18 sweets equally between 6 plates.

How many sweets on each plate?

★ Challenge

Isla has made brownies and wants to share them fairly with her friends. She has 19 brownies to share between 4 children.

How can she share them fairly?

Show how you worked out your answer.

5.5 Finding equivalent fractions

1 Match the groups that have the same amount. Draw a line to show which shapes match.

2 Nuria makes three long shapes with playdough. She keeps one whole, cuts one into halves and the other into quarters.

1 whole

a) Draw a line to show where she would cut the playdough into halves.

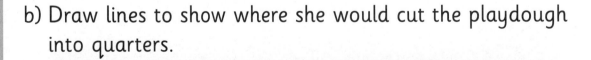

How many halves would she have? ☐

b) Draw lines to show where she would cut the playdough into quarters.

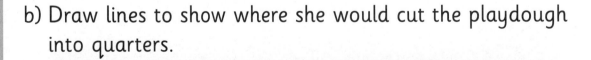

How many quarters would she have? ☐

3 These cakes have been cut in half. Draw lines to cut each whole cake into quarters.

a)

How many halves? ☐

How many quarters? ☐

b)

How many halves? ☐

How many quarters? ☐

c)

How many halves? ☐

How many quarters? ☐

d)

How many halves? ☐

How many quarters? ☐

★ **Challenge**

Isla has two whole sandwiches.   Finlay has one and a half sandwiches.

Nuria has eight quarter sandwiches.   Amman has four half sandwiches.

Which children have the same amount?

Draw a picture to show how you worked it out.

1 Share the food equally between Finlay and Nuria so that they each have half.

a)

One half of 6 cupcakes is [   ] cupcakes.

b)

One half of 10 biscuits is [   ] biscuits.

c)

One half of 14 grapes is [   ] grapes.

d)

One half of 8 brownies is [   ] brownies.

2 Share these foods equally between Amman, Isla, Finlay and Nuria so that they each have one quarter.

a)

One quarter of 12 strawberries is [ ] strawberries.

b)

One quarter of 8 oranges is [ ] oranges.

c)

One quarter of 16 sweets is [ ] sweets.

d)

One quarter of 24 blueberries is [ ] blueberries.

3 a) Amman has 22 chocolate buttons. He gives half the buttons to Finlay. How many chocolate buttons does he have left?

b) Finlay has 16 pennies. He puts one quarter in his piggy bank. How many pennies are in the piggy bank?

c) Isla has 20 marbles. How many marbles in one quarter?

d) Amman has 18 pencils. How many pencils in one half?

Challenge

Isla shares out muffins for snack between herself, Amman, Nuria and Finlay.

She has two muffins left on her plate. This is one quarter of all the muffins.

How many muffins did Isla start with? You could draw a picture to help you.

6.1 Making amounts

1 Draw lines to match each coin in the box to the set with the same value.

2 a) Draw coins to show two different ways to make 10p.

b) Can you make 10p another way? Draw the coins you could use.

22

3 a) Draw three coins to make 15p.

b) Draw four coins to make 20p.

c) Draw two different ways you could make 16p.

★ **Challenge**

Isla has 50p in her piggy bank. Can you think up four different ways to make 50p? Draw them on the Think Board.

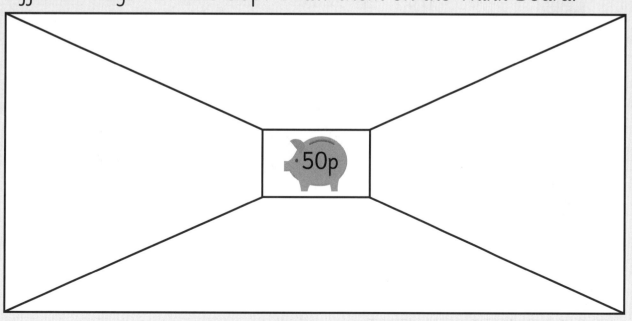

6.2 Adding amounts

1 How much altogether?

a) add = [　　　]

b) add = [　　　]

c) add add = [　　　]

d) add add =

e) add add add = [　　　]

2 How much does Isla need to pay in total for each group of items for snack?

SNACK

toast   10p

juice   12p

apple   8p

banana   9p

a)

b)

[　　　]

[　　　]

c)

d)

[　　　]

[　　　]

3 Isla has drawn coins to make 18p.

a) Can you think of another way to make 18p? Draw the coins here:

b) Who used the least number of coins?

Isla ☐   Me ☐

★ **Challenge**

Nuria has worked out the answers to these adding problems. Is she correct?

You could use coins or counting objects to help you.

✓   ✗

a) 12p + 9p = 20p   ☐

b) 5p + 14p = 19p   ☐

c) 11p + 5p + 7p = 23p   ☐

d) 9p + 10p + 5p + 5p = 30p   ☐

1 Amman and Isla are playing Shops. Amman says each marble costs 1p. Isla has a 10p coin.

Draw Isla's change from 10p when she buys each amount of marbles.

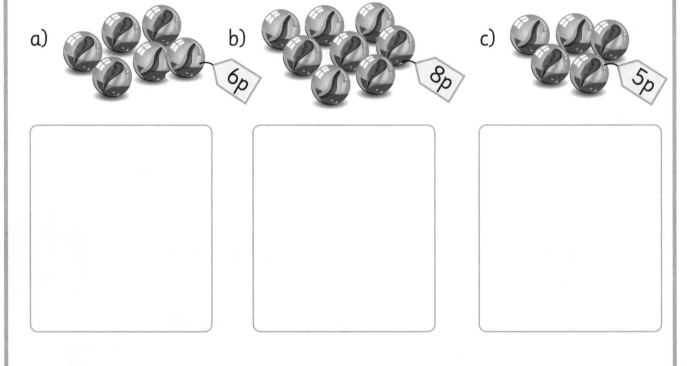

a) 6p

b) 8p

c) 5p

d)  1p

e)  3p

2 This time Isla has a 20p coin. Draw the change she will get if she spends these amounts.

a) 18p

b) 14p

c) 15p

d) 9p

f) 3p

3 Finlay spends 12p. How much change would he get if he paid with these coins?

a)

b)

c)

Finlay and Nuria both had 20p coins. They each spent some money at the shop.

a) Finlay has these coins left.

How much money did Finlay spend?

How much change did he get?

b) Nuria has these coins left.

How much money did Nuria spend?

How much change did she get?

c) Who spent more, Finlay or Nuria?

Share with a partner how you worked each answer out.

1 Fill in the missing days of the week.

Monday

Wednesday

Saturday

2

	Teacher	Games	Practice
Monday	▲	●	▢
Tuesday	▢	▲	●
Wednesday	●	▢	▲
Thursday	▲	●	▢
Friday	▢	▲	●

a) Which group is with the teacher on Monday?

b) What do the Yellow Squares do on Wednesday?

c) What day do the Green Triangles have Practice?

d) Which days do the Blue Circles have Games?

	Monday	Tuesday	Wednesday	Thursday	Friday
9:00–10:30	Free Play	Numeracy	Free Play	Free Play	Literacy
10:30–10:45	Break	Break	Break	Break	Break
10:45–12:00	Numeracy	P.E.	Numeracy	Numeracy	Numeracy
12:00–1:00	Lunch	Lunch	Lunch	Lunch	Lunch
1:00–2:00	Literacy	Literacy	Literacy	Literacy	P.E.
2:00–3:00	Art	Music	RME	Assembly	Free Play

a) What comes first on Monday?

b) What time is Free Play on Friday?

c) What comes after Literacy on Thursday?

Complete the calendar for Isla's after school activities.

Monday	Tuesday		Thursday	
		Basketball		free day

On Tuesday Isla has Rainbows.

She plays basketball on Wednesdays.

Isla has Jigsaw Club on Mondays.

Dancing is every Thursday.

Isla has a free day every Friday.

1 Draw a line to match the activity with the best unit of time.

blink three times   minutes

go to the beach   days

draw a picture   hours

grow cress   seconds

2 Colour the best unit of time to measure these activities.

a) Take a long walk

(hours) (days) (seconds) (minutes)

b) Draw a circle

(hours) (days) (seconds) (minutes)

c) Play a board game

(hours) (days) (seconds) (minutes)

d) Go on holiday

(hours) (days) (seconds) (minutes)

3 What would work best to time these activities? Colour the one you think would work best.

a) Do four star jumps

b) Tidy up the classroom

c) Watch a film

d) Find out how long until the Summer holidays

★ **Challenge**

Work with a partner.

a) Estimate how many of each activity you think you could do in **one minute**.

b) Use a stopwatch to find out how many of each you can actually do!

	Estimate	Actual number
Hop on one leg		
Write your name		
Pass a ball between you and a partner		
Say all the letters in the alphabet		

1 Draw the hour hand on the clocks for each of these times.

a) 6 o'clock

b) 8 o'clock

c) 11 o'clock

d) Half past 5

e) Half past 2

f) Half past 11

2 Match each clock to the correct time.

a)   b)    c)    d)    e)

half past 4   half past 7   half past 12   3 o'clock   12 o'clock

3 Write the time shown on each clock.

a)

b)

c)

4 Draw the hour hand and minute hand on each clock to show these times.

a) 7 o'clock

b) half past 1

c) half past 3

★ **Challenge**

Nuria's teacher asked her to write the time shown on each clock. Put a tick in the box if Nuria is correct and put a cross if she has made a mistake.

a)

Three o'clock ☐

b)

Half past ten ☐

c)

Eleven o'clock ☐

d)

Half past two ☐

1 Draw lines to match the times.

a)
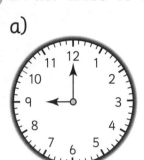

b)
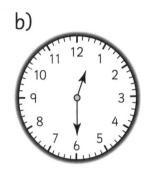

c)

d)
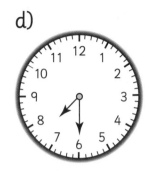

| 11:00 | 7:30 | 12:30 | 9:00 |

2 Fill in the missing numbers to make each digital clock match the analogue clock above it.

a)

b)

c)

d)

e)

| :00 | 3: | :30 | : | : |

3 Draw hands on each analogue clock so that it matches the digital clock.

a)

b)

c)

d)

e)
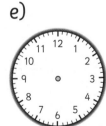

| 10:00 | 4:30 | 9:30 | 7:30 | 12:00 |

Nuria thinks the analogue clock shows this time:

1:30

Finlay thinks it shows this time:

12:30

a) Who is correct?

How do you know?

b) Draw hands on the first clock to show Nuria's guess.
    Draw hands on the second clock to show Finlay's guess.

8.1 Comparing and ordering lengths and heights

1 Circle the **longer** object in each pair.

a)

b)

c)

d)

2 Circle the **shortest** object in each set.

a)

b)

c)

d)

e)

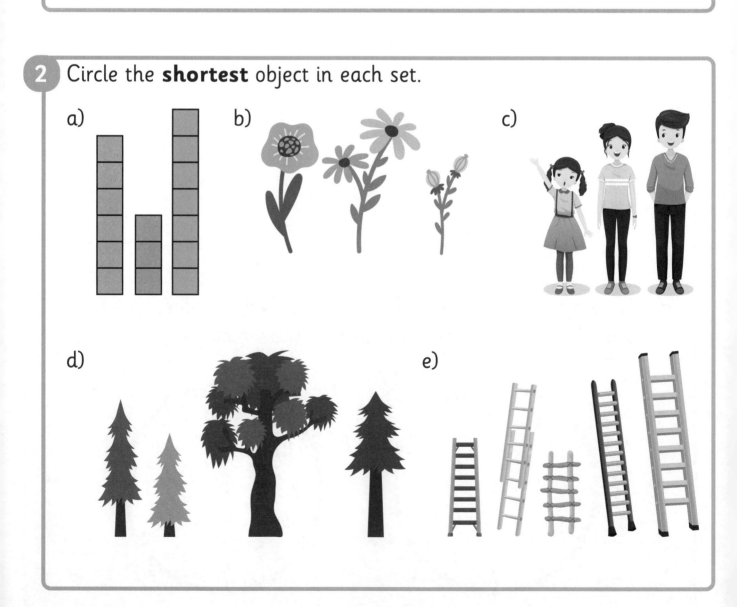

3 Draw these objects in order from shortest to tallest. Make the smallest object number 1 and the longest object number 5.

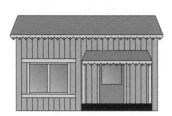

a) Draw a snake that is longer than this one.

b) Draw an animal that is shorter than the elephant.

c) Draw a flower that is shorter than this one.

d) Draw a tree that is taller than this one.

1 Draw the **heavier** object each time.

a)

b)

c)

d)

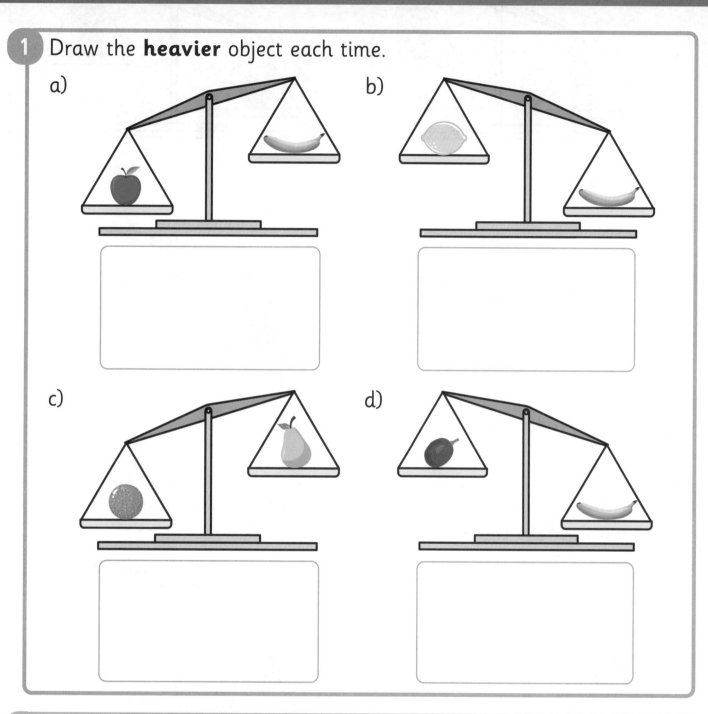

2 Work out the **lightest** object each time. Use the pictures to help you.

a)

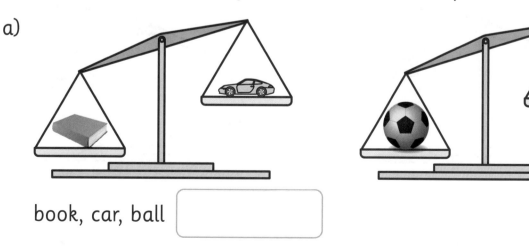

book, car, ball

b)

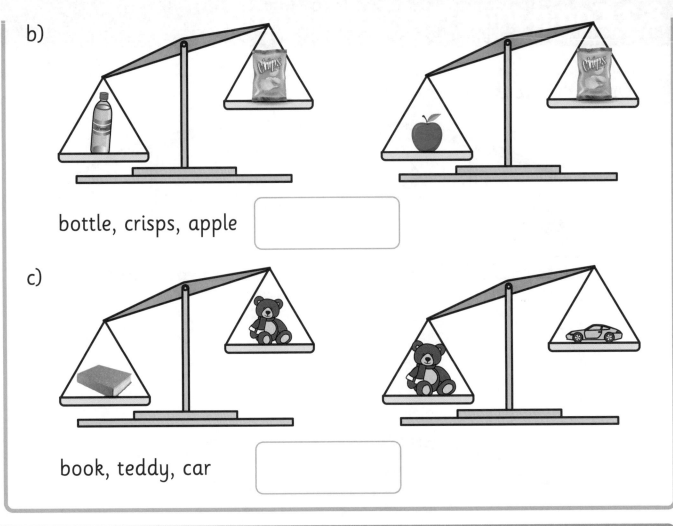

bottle, crisps, apple

c)

book, teddy, car

---

3 Use the pictures to help you order these objects from lightest to heaviest. Make the lightest object number 1.

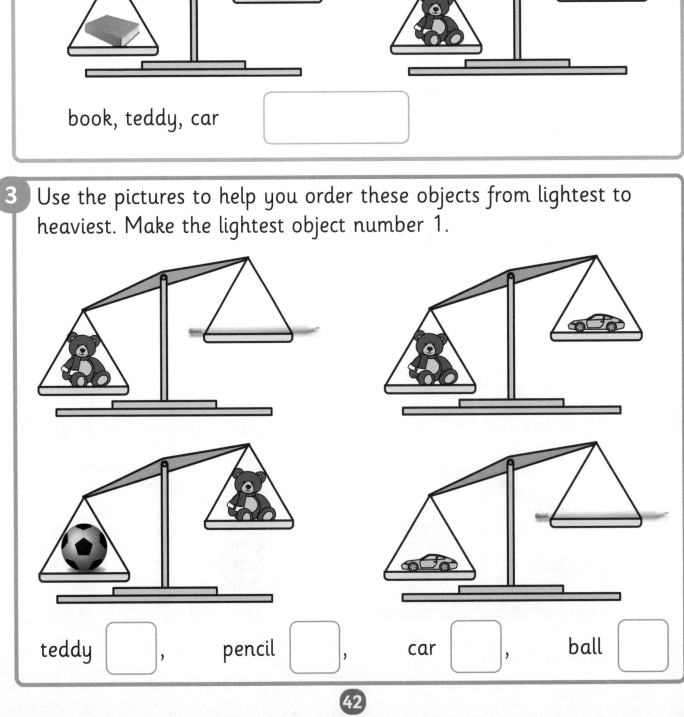

teddy ___, pencil ___, car ___, ball ___

a)

Amman thinks he is heavier than Isla. Is he correct?

How do you know?

b)

Is Amman heavier than Finlay?

How do you know?

c)

Who is the lightest of all the children?

How do you know?

1 Tick the **largest** paddling pool.

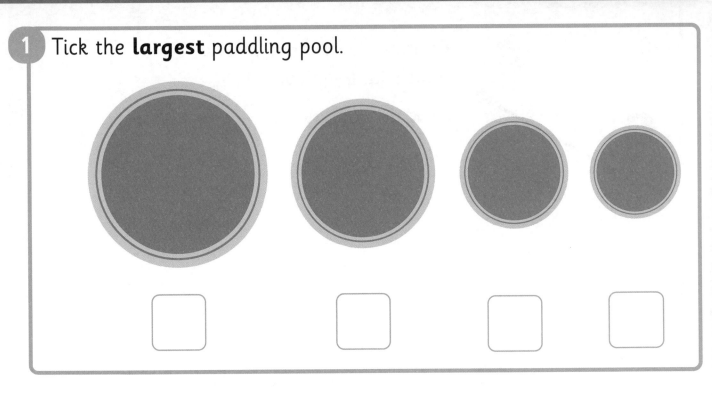

2 The children are painting.

Amman

Isla

Finlay

Nuria

Who has the largest piece of paper?

Who has the smallest piece of paper?

3 Number each kite in order of size from smallest to largest.
Make the smallest kite number 1.

★ **Challenge**

a) Draw a park with a larger area than this one.

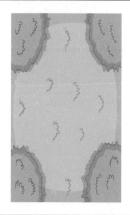

b) Draw a pool with a smaller area than this one.

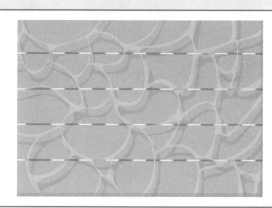

1 Tick the object which would hold the **least** amount of water.

a)

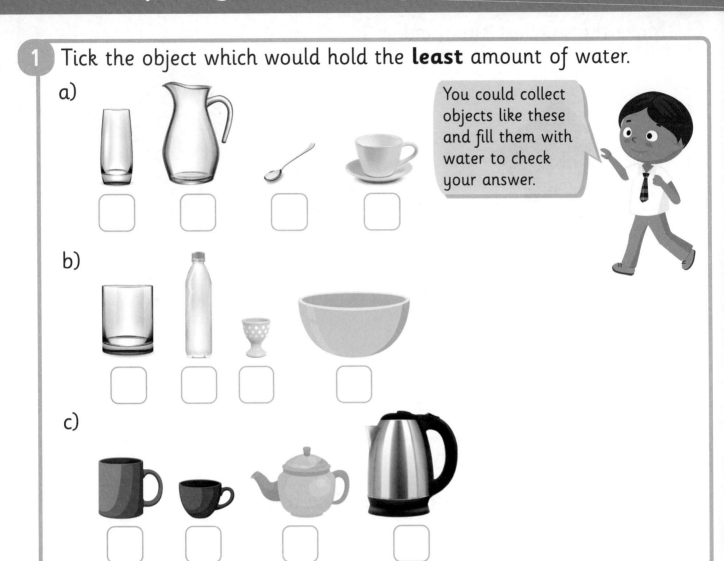

You could collect objects like these and fill them with water to check your answer.

b)

c)

2 Tick the object that would hold the **most** sand.

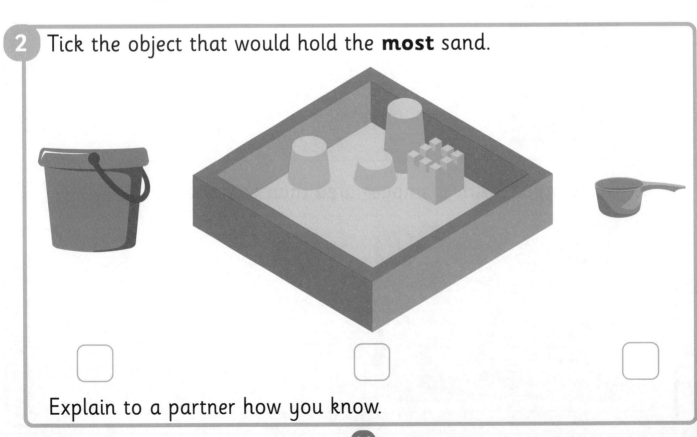

Explain to a partner how you know.

3 Order these objects from the smallest to largest capacity.

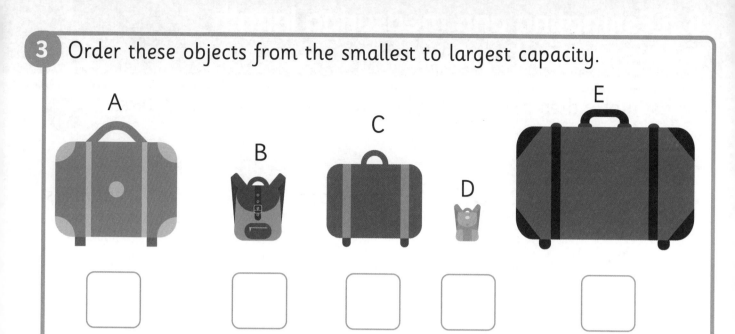

A   B   C   D   E

☐   ☐   ☐   ☐   ☐

★ Challenge

Amman says the bottle contains more water than the bowl because the level is higher. Nuria thinks the bowl holds more water.

Who do you agree with? [   ]

Explain your answer to a partner. You could use similar containers to help you.

8.5 Estimating and measuring length (non-standard units)

1 Estimate, then measure the length of each shoe in counters.

a)

Estimate: [ ] counters

Actual length: [ ] counters

b)

Estimate: [ ] counters

Actual length: [ ] counters

c)

Estimate: [ ] counters

Actual length: [ ] counters

d)

Estimate: [ ] counters

Actual length: [ ] counters

Finlay and Isla make paper aeroplanes.
They throw them and use their feet to
measure how far their planes fly.

Work with a partner to make two paper planes.

Take turns to throw them from the same start point.

a) Now use **your** feet to measure how far each aeroplane flew.

My plane: [   ] feet.   My partner's plane: [   ] feet.

b) Measure again using **your partner's** feet.

My plane: [   ] feet.   My partner's plane: [   ] feet.

c) Are the measurements the same?   [   ]

d) If your teacher measured using their feet would their answer
    be the same?   [   ]

    Talk to your partner about why the answers might be different.

e) What else could you use to measure the length of each throw?

    [   ]

    Work with your partner to investigate different ways to
    measure how far each plane flew.

1 How many blocks weigh the same as these items?

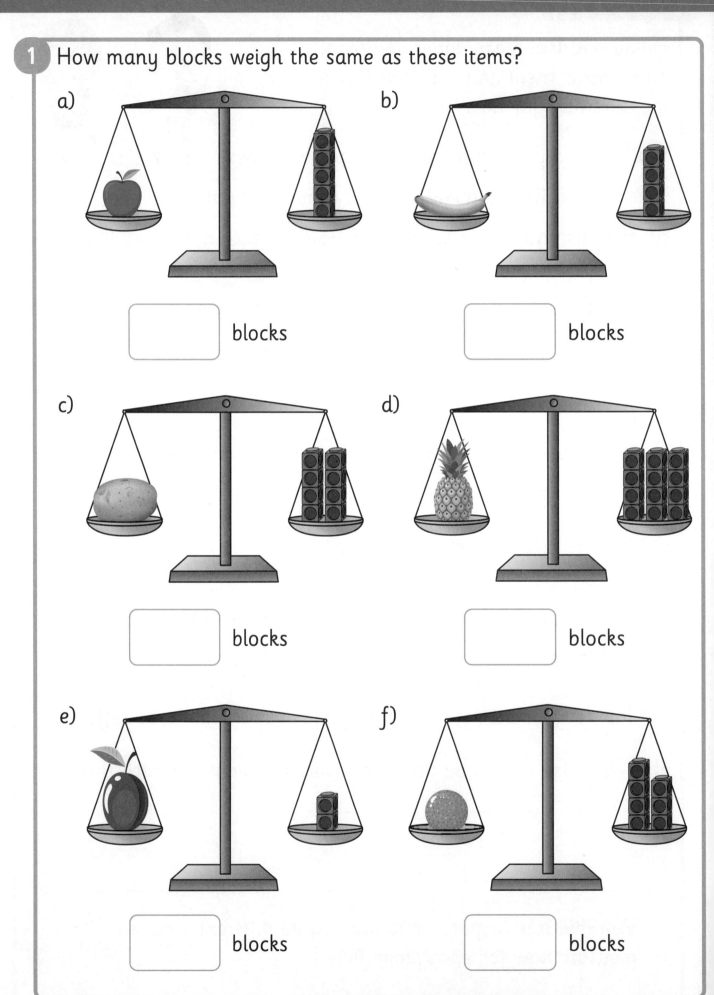

a)

_____ blocks

b)

_____ blocks

c)

_____ blocks

d)

_____ blocks

e)

_____ blocks

f)

_____ blocks

2 Isla has been using cubes to find the mass of these items. Which item weighs the **most**?

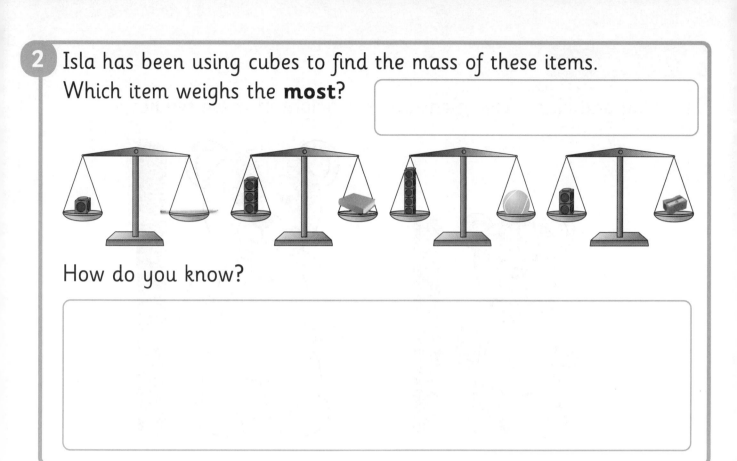

How do you know?

3 Amman has been using pencils to weigh these items. Tick the item that weighs the **least**.

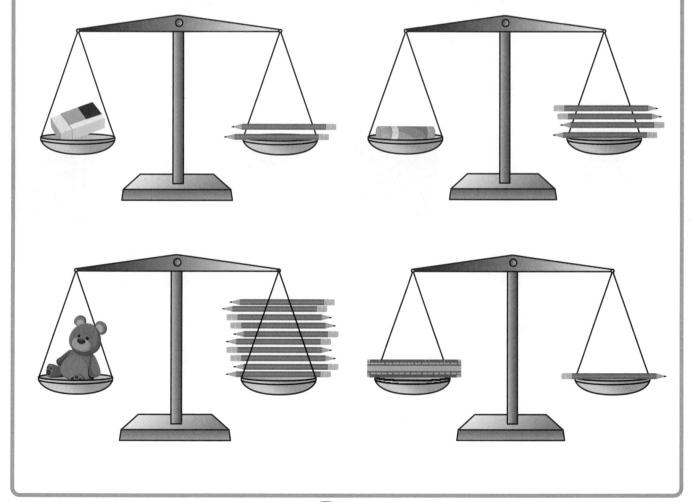

Finlay and Nuria have measured the height of these teddies.

Now they want to measure how heavy they are.

Finlay thinks the blue teddy will be heavier because it is taller.
Do you agree? Talk with a partner about your ideas.

The children use cubes to weigh the teddies.

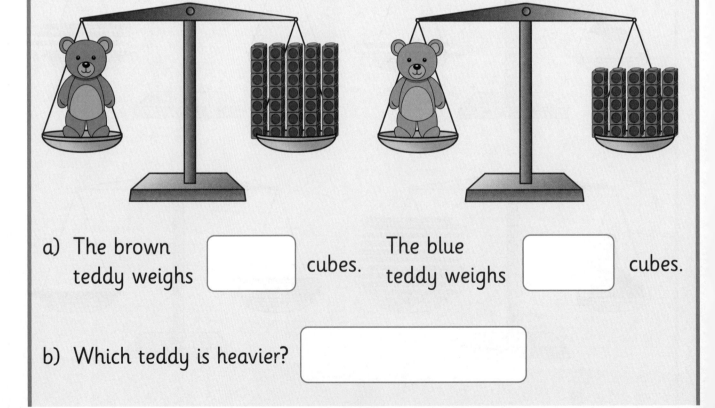

a) The brown
    teddy weighs ⬜ cubes.

The blue
teddy weighs ⬜ cubes.

b) Which teddy is heavier? ⬜

c) Now pick some different toys to weigh. You will need a pan balance and some things to measure with. You could use cubes, blocks or any other small items.

Work with a partner. Draw a picture of the toys you have picked in the first column.

Toy	Estimate	Mass

d) Estimate how heavy you think each toy will be. Write or draw your estimate in the second column.

e) Now weigh each toy. Write or draw each toy's weight in the third column.

1

a) Estimate how many circular plates will fit side-by-side onto this table.

About _____ plates

b) Estimate how many rectangular place mats are needed to cover this table.

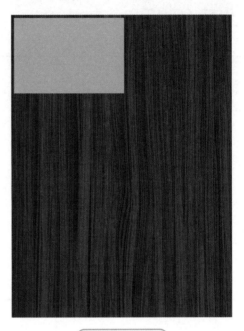

About _____ place mats

c) Estimate how many triangular napkins are needed to cover this table.

About _____ napkins

d) Estimate how many square drinks mats are needed to cover this whole table.

About _____ drinks mats.

2 Use cubes, counters or other small objects to measure how many would fit onto these pieces of paper.

a)

b)

c)

a) Estimate how many of your handprints will fit this box.

How many of your handprints fit in the box?

b) You will need a piece of paper with the same area as your workbook. Paint your hand and print the paper with your handprints to measure the area. Be careful to use all the space to fit in as many as you can. Try not to overlap!

Talk to a partner and find out if they have the same answer. If it is different, why might that be?

Try not to leave any gaps between your fingers!

1 Estimate how many cups of water will fill up the jug.
Tick the answer you think is correct.

2 Estimate how many buckets of water will fill up a paddling pool.
Tick the answer you think is correct.

5 buckets ☐

2 buckets ☐

7 buckets ☐

15 buckets ☐

3

a) Estimate how many cups it will take to fill the small bucket with sand.

About [ ] cups

b) Estimate how many scoops it will take to fill the big bucket with sand.

About [ ] scoops

c) Estimate how many measuring spoons it will take to fill the bowl with sand.

About [ ] spoons

d) Estimate how many bags it will take to fill the sandpit with sand.

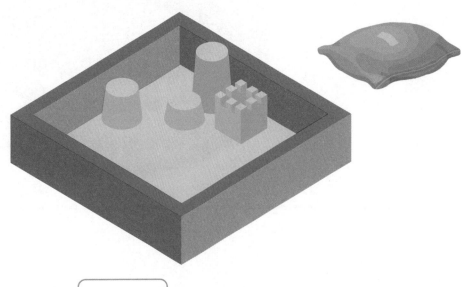

About [ ] bags

Work with a partner. Find three different containers. Now choose a small pot or cup to fill up your containers with water.

a) Draw a picture of each container in the first column.

Container	Estimate	Capacity

b) Talk to your partner about which container you think will hold the most. Put a tick beside it.

c) Estimate how many of your cups will fill up each container. Write or draw your estimates in the second column.

d) Now use your cup to fill up each container. Count how many and write or draw in the third column.

Talk to your partner about your answers.

1 Circle all the numbers you can see in the picture.

2 Look at the scoreboards. Which teams are winning?

a)

RED 12 19 GREEN

b)

BLUE 21 20 RED

c)

ORANGE 41 14 GREEN

3 Isla is making playdough.

PLAYDOUGH

2 cups of water

2 cups of flour

2 tablespoons of oil

1 cup of salt

4 teaspoons of Cream of Tartar

5 drops of food colouring

Directions:

Mix together in a large bowl.

a) How many cups of flour does Isla need?

b) How much salt does she need?

c) How much food colouring does she need?

d) How much oil does she need?

You could have a go at making playdough using this or another recipe!

Work with a partner. Talk about your day so far. Can you think of all the ways you used numbers from when you woke up in the morning until now?

Draw or write them here:

10.1 Continuing patterns

1 Draw and colour the shape that comes next.

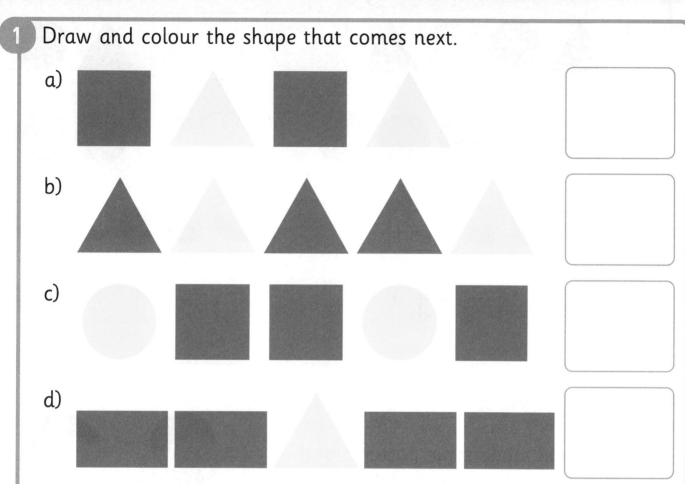

a)

b)

c)

d)

2 Continue these patterns.

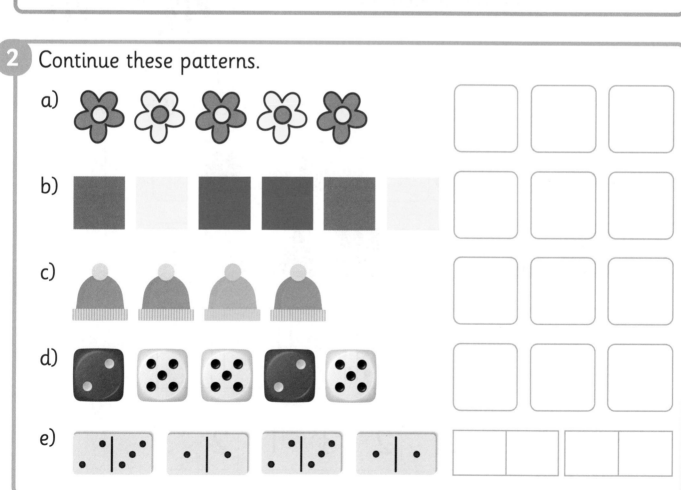

a)

b)

c)

d)

e)

3 Complete the missing parts of each pattern.

a)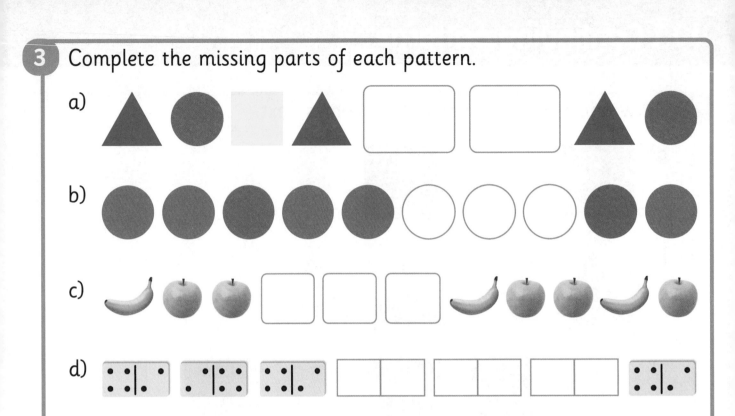

b)

c)

d)

---

1. Amman made some patterns and Finlay tried to continue them. Is Finlay right?

a) Put a tick if the pattern is correct and a cross if it is wrong.

i)

ii)

iii)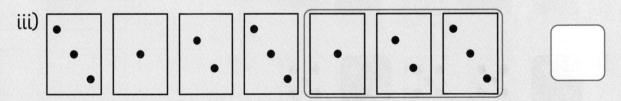

iv) 1 2 3 1 2 3 1 2 3

b) Here are the patterns again. Try to continue them.

i)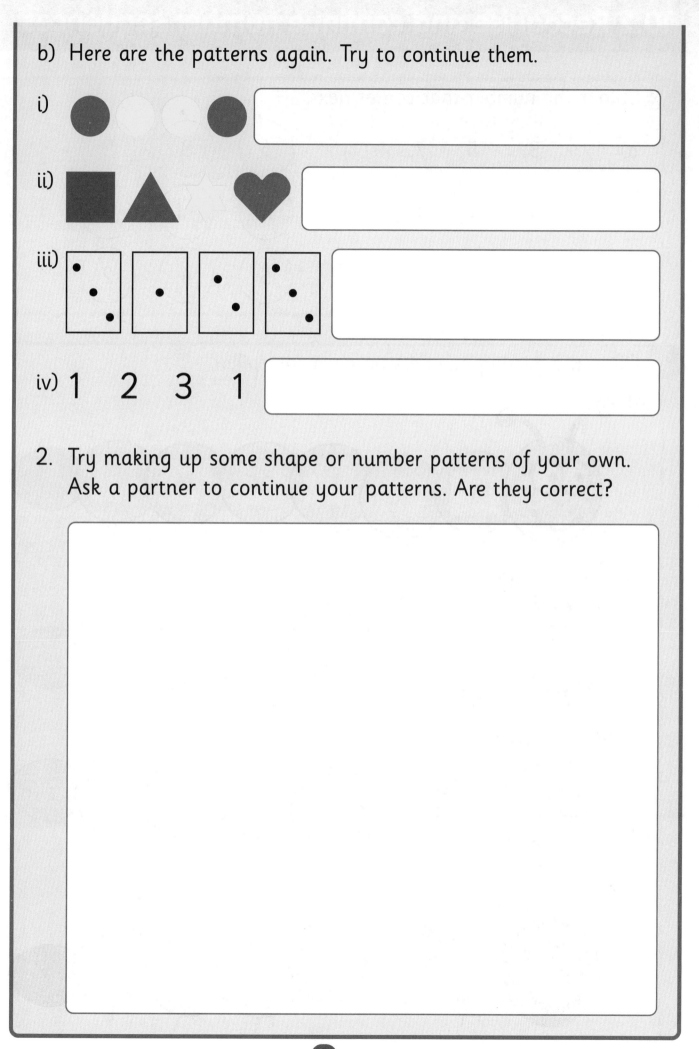

ii)

iii)

iv) 1   2   3   1

2. Try making up some shape or number patterns of your own.
   Ask a partner to continue your patterns. Are they correct?

1 Colour the number that comes next.

a) 1,   3,   5,   7,   (6) (8) (9)

b) 1,   4,   7,   10,   (13) (11) (14)

c) 12,   10,   8,   6,   (5) (4) (2)

2 Fill in the missing numbers on each caterpillar.

a)

5   10   15   20   25   [ ]

b)

6   10   14   18   [ ]   [ ]

c)

24   21   18   15   [ ]   [ ]

d)

21   19   17   15   [ ]   [ ]

3 Fill in the missing numbers.

a) 4   7   10   [ ]   [ ]   19   22

b) 21   19   [ ]   [ ]   [ ]   11   9

c) 90   80   [ ]   [ ]   [ ]   [ ]   30   20

d) 6   11   16   [ ]   [ ]   [ ]   [ ]   41   46

★ **Challenge**

The children have each come up with a number sequence.
Can you explain the pattern for each one?

4, 8, 12, 16, 20, 24, 28

a) Finlay's number sequence is [ ]

89, 84, 79, 74, 69, 64, 59, 54, 49, 44

b) Isla's number sequence is [ ]

Can you make up your own number sequence? Ask a partner to guess the pattern.

[ ]

1 Write a number sentence for each domino.

a)

[ ] + [ ] = [ ]

b)

[ ] + [ ] = [ ]

c)

[ ] + [ ] = [ ]

d)

[ ] + [ ] = [ ]

2 How many dots must be on the other side of each ladybird? Complete these number sentences. You could draw spots to help you.

a)

8 + [ ] = 12

b)

[ ] + 5 = 14

c)

12 − [ ] = 7

d)

15 = 11 + [ ]

3 Write the missing number or symbol for each number sentence.

a) 6 ☐ 8 = 14

b) 9 = 11 − ☐

c) 12 + ☐ = 16

d) 12 = 3 ☐ 9

e) 17 − ☐ = 12

f) 9 = 18 ☐ 9

★ **Challenge**

Both sides of the pan balance equal 14. Think up two different number sentences that equal 14 and write them in each part of the pan balance. You could use objects or draw pictures to help you.

a) ☐ + ☐   ☐ + ☐   b) ☐ + ☐   ☐ + ☐

c) ☐ − ☐   ☐ − ☐   d) ☐ − ☐   ☐ − ☐

Write four different number sentences that equal 14 here. You could use addition or subtraction.

Share with a partner. Did they come up with different number sentences?

12.1 2D shapes

1 Draw lines to match each shape to the correct name.

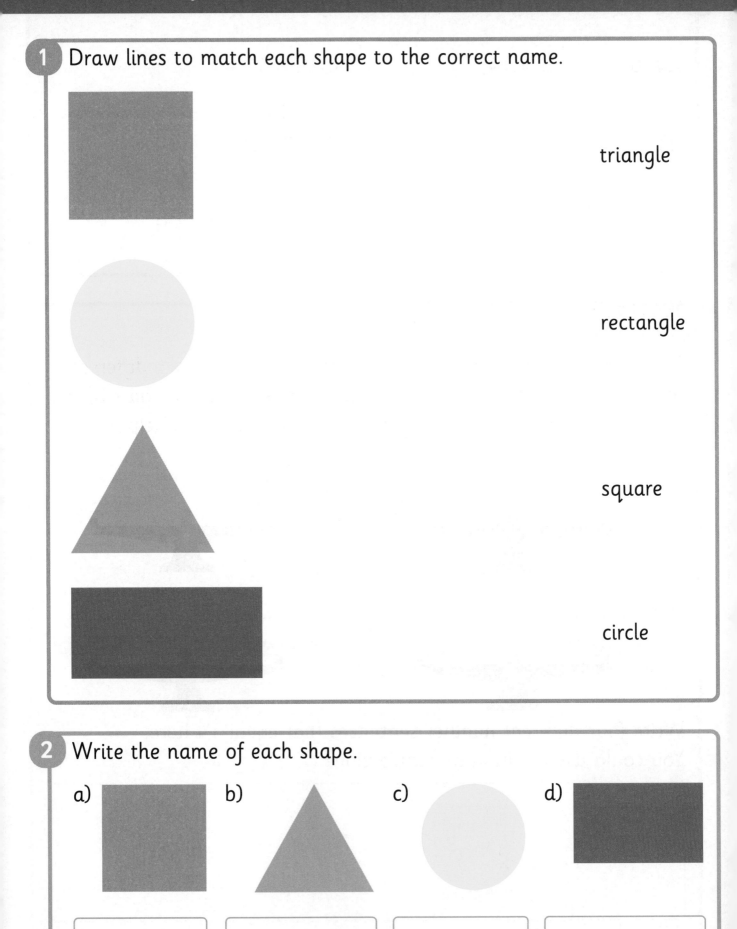

triangle

rectangle

square

circle

2 Write the name of each shape.

a) b) c) d)

3

- Colour all the circles blue.
- Colour all the rectangles red.
- Colour all the triangles green.
- Colour all the squares yellow.

★ **Challenge**

a) Draw a shape that has three sides.

I have drawn a _____

b) Draw a shape that is round.

I have drawn a _____

c) Draw a shape with two long sides and two short sides.

I have drawn a _____

d) Draw a shape that has four sides all the same length.

I have drawn a _____

12.2 Sorting 2D shapes

1 How many corners does each shape have?

a)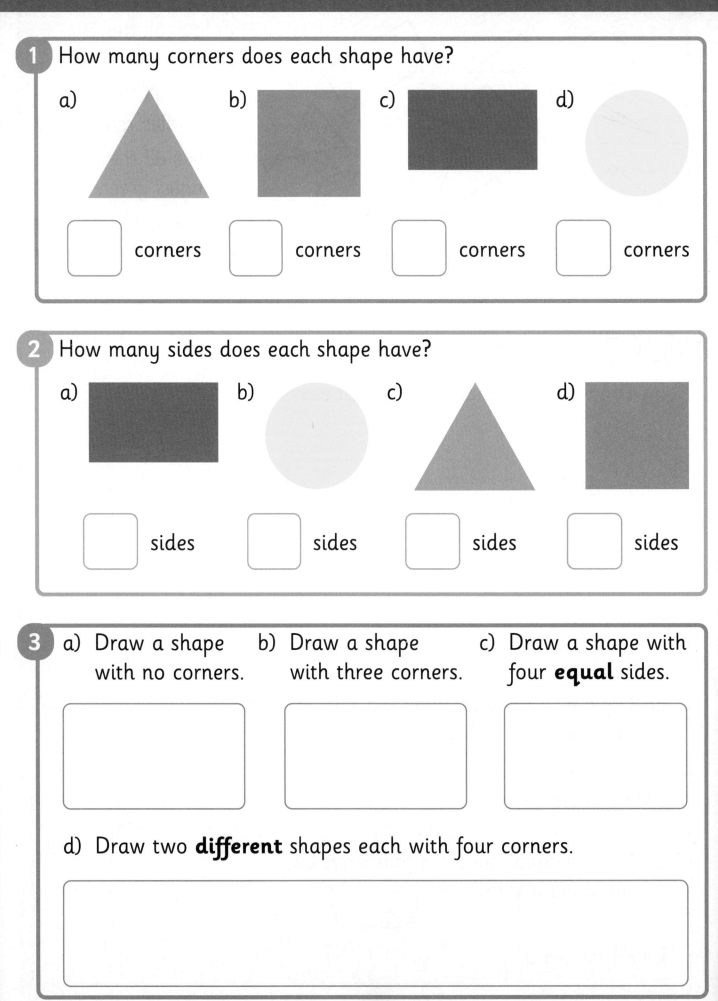

☐ corners

b)

☐ corners

c)

☐ corners

d)

☐ corners

2 How many sides does each shape have?

a)

☐ sides

b)

☐ sides

c)

☐ sides

d)

☐ sides

3 a) Draw a shape with no corners.

b) Draw a shape with three corners.

c) Draw a shape with four **equal** sides.

d) Draw two **different** shapes each with four corners.

4 Tick the shape that's the odd one out. Explain to a partner why.

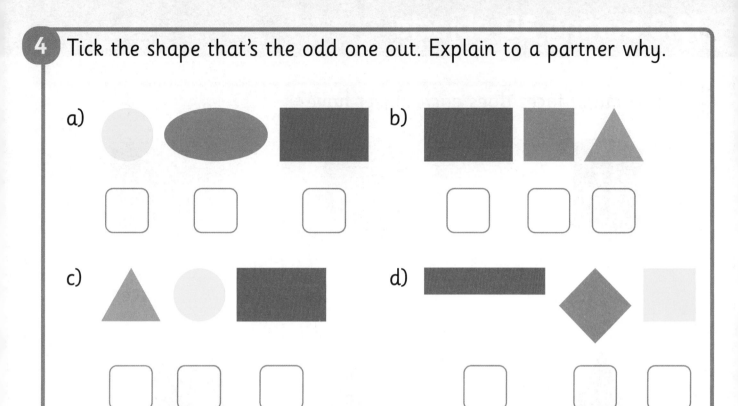

a)

b)

c)

d)

★ **Challenge**

Think up a rule to sort these shapes into the two hoops, then draw each shape in the correct hoop.

Talk to a partner. Can they guess the rule you used to sort the shapes?

1 How many faces does each object have?

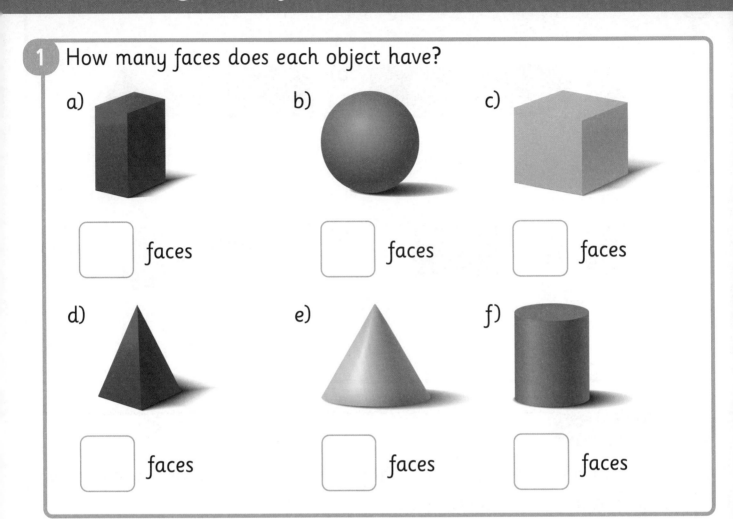

a)

☐ faces

b)

☐ faces

c)

☐ faces

d)

☐ faces

e)

☐ faces

f)

☐ faces

2 Colour all the objects that have a curved face.

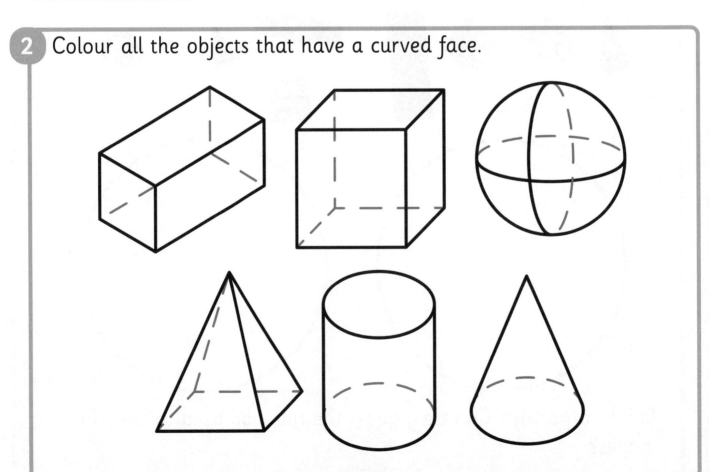

3 Tick the object that is the odd one out. Explain your answers to a partner.

a)

☐   ☐   ☐

b)

☐   ☐   ☐

c)

☐   ☐   ☐

d)

☐   ☐   ☐

Look around you. Can you find these 3D objects?

Draw them in the table below.

A 3D object with one curved face	
A 3D object with a curved face and a flat face	
A 3D object with no corners	
Three different 3D objects with more than five faces	

1 Write the name to match each 3D object. Choose from:

| cone | cube | sphere |

| cuboid | square-based pyramid | cylinder |

a)

b)

c)

d)

e)

f)

2 Draw lines to match each 3D object to the correct number of faces. You could use actual 3D objects to help you.

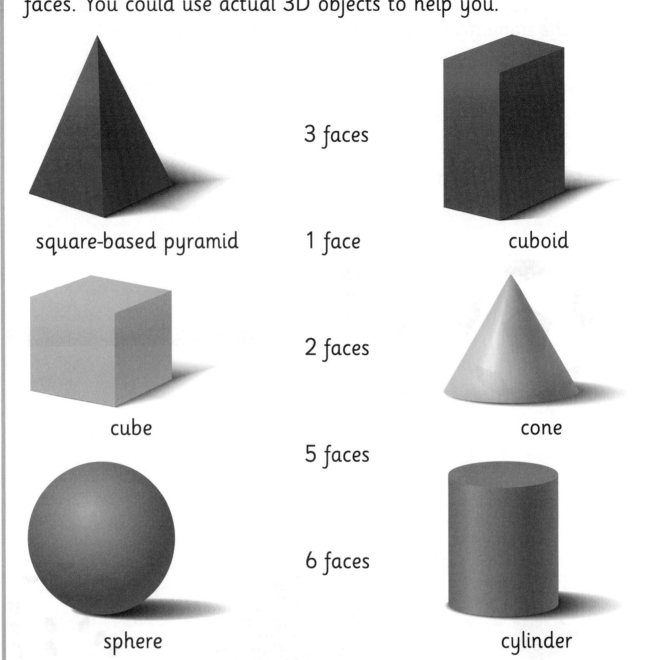

square-based pyramid

3 faces

1 face

cuboid

cube

2 faces

cone

5 faces

6 faces

sphere

cylinder

3 a) Colour the 3D objects that have eight corners.

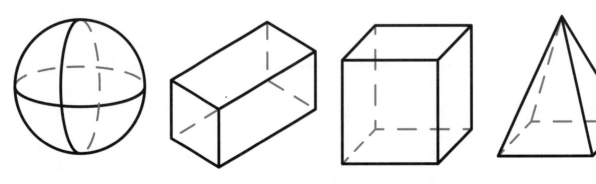

b) Colour the 3D object that has two edges.

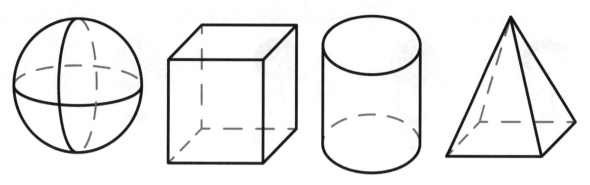

★ Challenge

Amman is playing Guess the 3D object with Isla. Help Isla to solve Amman's clues.

Draw and write your answers in the boxes.

a) It has six faces.
   They are all square.

b) It has one round flat face.
   It has one corner.

c) It has no corners.
   It has no edges.

d) It has eight corners.
   It has six faces.
   Each face is a rectangle.

1

Finlay   Nuria   Amman   Isla

a) Who is behind Finlay?

b) Who is between Nuria and Isla?

c) Who is in front of Isla?

d) Who is Nuria behind?

2

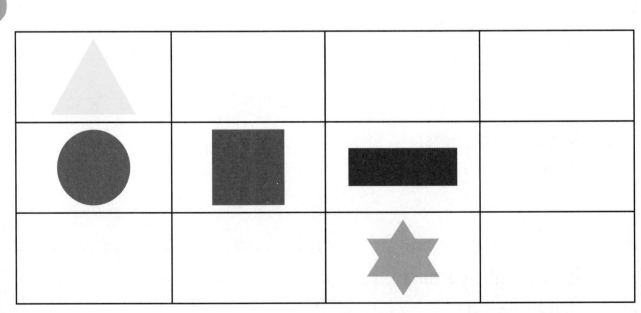

a) Draw and colour the shape that is above the

b) Draw and colour the shape that is to the right of the

c) Draw the shape that is to the left of the

d) Draw a yellow circle in the space below the red square.

This shape is _____ the orange star.

a) Follow the clues to find the treasure.

i) Draw a flag in the square above the pirate hat.

ii) Draw a volcano in the square to the left of your flag.

iii) Draw a house below your volcano.

iv) Draw an **X** below your house – you have found the treasure!

b) Work with a partner to make your own treasure map on squared paper and write some clues.

Give your clues to another pair. Can they find your treasure?

1 Here is a plan of a car park. Use a counter to help you follow the directions.

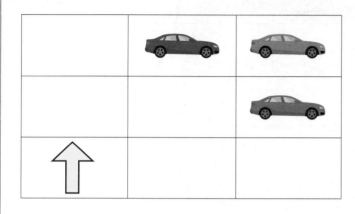 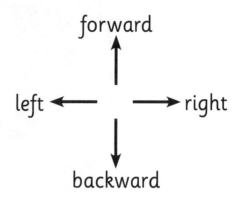

a) Start at the arrow. Go forward 2 squares and right 1 square.

Draw and colour the car in the square you are at.

b) Start at the arrow. Go forward 1 square and right 2 squares.

Draw and colour the car in the square you are at.

c) Start at the arrow. Go forward 2 squares and right 2 squares.

Draw the car in the square you are at.

2 Here is a treasure map. Can you give the pirates directions to find the treasure?

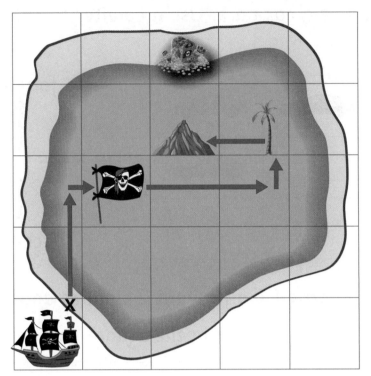

a) Start at the ship. Go to the flag.

How many squares forward? ⬚

How many squares right? ⬚

b) Start at the flag. Go to the tree.

⬚ squares right

⬚ squares forward.

c) Start at the tree. Go to the mountain.

⬚ squares ⬚

d) Draw a line to the treasure.

⬚ squares ⬚

Isla wants to visit Amman.

She needs to get from her house to his. Isla's mum says she can go by herself as long as she doesn't walk on or cross the road.

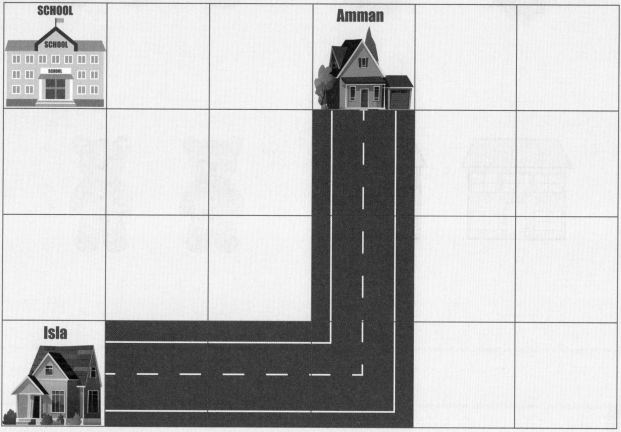

Draw a path on the map for Isla to walk on, then write the directions here:

Share with a partner. Did they go the same way as you?

13.3 Symmetry

1 Tick the symmetrical picture in each pair.

a)

☐ ☐

b)

☐ ☐

c)

☐ ☐

d)

☐ ☐

2 Draw the other side of each picture to make it symmetrical.

a)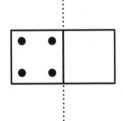

b)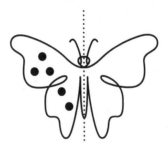

c)

d)

e)

f)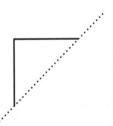

3 Complete each pattern so that it is symmetrical.

a)

b)

c)

d)

e)

f)

⭐ **Challenge**

Draw the lines of symmetry on these pictures. There may be more than one!

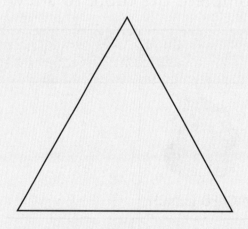

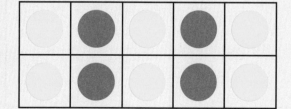

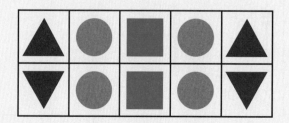

1 Isla sorts cubes into different colours. Complete the table.

COLOURS	TALLY	TOTAL
■ (black cube)	卌 卌 卌 卌 卌	
■ (grey cube)	卌 卌 卌 |||	
□ (white cube)	卌 卌 卌 卌 ||||	
■ (dark grey cube)	卌 卌 卌 卌 卌 |||	

2 Finlay is counting lunch numbers for his class.

12 children are having packed lunch.

16 children are having school lunch.

Complete the table to show this information.

	TALLY	TOTAL
PACKED LUNCH		
SCHOOL LUNCH		

3 Nuria finds out who has pets in her class. Use tally marks to record this information then write the total number of each pet.

PET	TALLY	TOTAL

⭐ **Challenge**

Work with a partner. Take turns to see how many star jumps you each can do in 30 seconds.

Record how many using tally marks then complete the table.

	TALLY	TOTAL
ME		
PARTNER		

Who did more star jumps?

Try thinking up some other activities to record using tally marks.

1 The children in Amman's class tried apples and grapes
to see which was their favourite.

	Favourite fruit									
Apples	🍎	🍎	🍎	🍎	🍎					
Grapes	🍇	🍇	🍇	🍇	🍇	🍇	🍇	🍇	🍇	
	1	2	3	4	5	6	7	8	9	10

a) How many children liked apples best?

b) How many children liked grapes best?

c) Which was the favourite, apples or grapes?

2 Here is a chart showing the month each child in P2 was born.

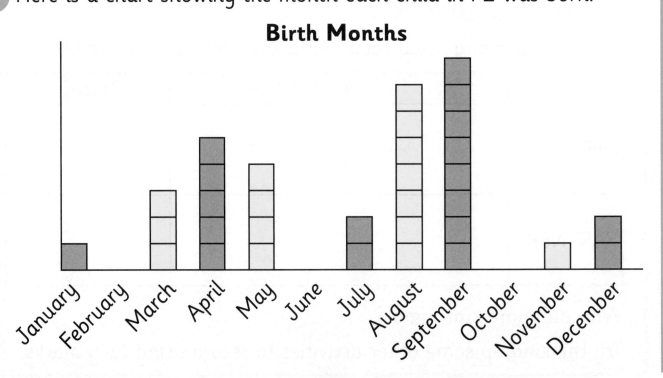

Birth Months

a) In which month were most P2 children born?

b) How many children were born in July?

c) Were more children born in May or March?

Isla's class voted on their favourite colour. They used counters to show their favourite colour on the graph.

Favourite Colours												
red	●	●										
pink	●	●	●	●	●	●	●	●				
orange	●											
yellow	○	○										
green	●	●	●	●	●	●	●	●	●			
blue	●	●	●	●	●	●						
	1	2	3	4	5	6	7	8	9	10		

Isla says green is the most popular colour.
Amman thinks pink is the most popular.

Who is right?

How do you know?

1 Nuria went shopping and bought some fruit. Here are all the different fruits she bought.

Draw the correct number of each fruit on this table.

Types of fruit	
🍌	
🍎	
🍐	
🍊	

Which fruit did Nuria buy most of?

2 Finlay does a survey to find out the eye colours of the children in his class.

Fill in the total for each eye colour using the tally marks.

Eye colour		Tally	Total
blue	👁	IIII IIII I	
brown	👁	IIII IIII IIII	
green	👁	IIII	

Now use the data to complete this bar chart.

	Eye colours					
15						
14						
13						
12						
11						
10						
9						
8						
7						
6						
5						
4						
3						
2						
1						

Number of children

blue   brown   green

a) Which eye colour is most common?

b) How many more children have brown
    eyes than blue eyes?

c) Look at the tally chart and the bar chart.
    Which is easier to read? Explain to a partner.

★ Challenge

Work with a partner. Pick some people to help with your survey and find out their favourite game. Make a bar chart to show your results.

15.1 Understanding chance

1 Draw lines to match each sentence with the correct word.

a) It will be sunny today   certain

b) A cow will jump over the moon   possible

c) The sun will set tonight   impossible

2 Tick the answer you think is correct.

a) The number after 15 is 16.

Certain ☐   Possible ☐

Impossible ☐

b) A week has 8 days.

Certain ☐   Possible ☐

Impossible ☐

c) Summer will be hot.

Certain ☐   Possible ☐

Impossible ☐

d) I will drop something.

Certain ☐   Possible ☐

Impossible ☐

e) At six o'clock, the small hand will point to six.

Certain ☐   Possible ☐

Impossible ☐

f) The clock will go backwards.

Certain ☐   Possible ☐

Impossible ☐

3 Isla rolls two 6-sided dice and adds the numbers together.

Look at each result. Are they: **certain**, **possible** or **impossible**? Write your answer in the box.

a) She rolls a total of 5.

b) She rolls a total of 1.

c) She rolls a total of 9.

d) She rolls a total of 14.

★ Challenge

Nuria tells Finlay about her day, but she makes up some things to trick him!

Can you find the impossible things? Tick the box for each sentence you think is **impossible**.

I got up at 9 o'clock and I was on time for school.

I liked maths this morning.

I had an apple for snack.

I learned that 10 is bigger than 100.

I had a sandwich for lunch.

I walked home on my bike.

Talk to a partner and make up some more sentences about things that are certain, possible or impossible in your day! Do you always agree?